FOG THE DOG

by

Jorge Silva

No dog or any other animal should be a victim of the harsh face of humankind.

This book is a work of fiction, I wish my dog could talk and use a language full of blasphemy, profanity and obscenity. The names, characters and incidents are product of the author's experiences and imagination.

Fog wakes up every day at the same time 5:30 am, to get ready to go to work, except on his days off. Well, he meditates, poops, showers and eats breakfast; Commutes to his job, does what Fog does best, then comes back home.

Wait! In the way back he stops at this cool café to get a cortado, so fucking good, have you have one? Then rushes because at 4:00 pm must be in the park exercising and killing those calories acquired at lunch; just after 5:00 pm he grabs a beer plays music and just completes any pending errands, reviews social media stuff, has dinner, makes love and goes to sleep, just like you and me. Every day the same exact routine, what a life. – Sigh.

If you asked me yes Fog the Dog is real, is a dog with big responsibilities, not like your old uncle who still pretends to be a teenager and embarrass you in front of your cool friends, Fog is the real deal a 6-year-old mix/mutt dog with a job, with qualities, issues and needs. Currently he is living at his parents (cough) in Los Angeles, but he certainly has a reason and that is to save enough money and buy a house in Florida where everything started.

1 The mission.

In an intergalactic base, a group of beings whom do not show themselves, are being heard talking about a launch.

"Sir. We are ready to launch project 3k." –Says the first voice.

"It was about time, it has been a while since we've received the first signal. This mission is so important, that is why we had to send the best trained cadet. He was so brave taking this task that we need to celebrate his bravery, does anyone have

mezcal?"

"I got tequila!" —A voice in the back yells.

"What? Tequila? Don't you know mezcal is the big

thing right now? Dude everywhere."

"What about vodka? I have vodka." —A second

member shouts.

"Are you kidding me vodka would kill me, I am

allergic to potatoes."

"Hold on let me check the ingredients, probably

was made from grains, no it says 100% potatoes

never mind."

—Suddenly a multicolor lighting shows in the main

screen.

"Attention! Stress and turbulence are incrementing, he is about to cross the gate, Sir, we are losing him, Sir, we need to abort." —Yells concerned.

"It's too late for that, we need to back him up, shoot the ultra-cosmic light, now!"

"It's dangerous the frame (body) is to fragile, it won't resist!"

"Let's believe in the universe and double that nasty ray, do it!"

—Lights started to go off and on while outside the shift, energy was being concentrated then shot directly to earth, where a big explosion came at contact, everyone waited in silence.

"I am receiving a signal he is in!" —Dub, dub, the sound of a heart beats started to fill the room, then the pop of a bottle of champagne opening in the

back.

"Great job! Is that champagne?"

"Yes, it is Sir!"

"Wait, was that made in France?"

"Let's see, it says Napa Valley!"

"To be name Champagne must come only from,

what a heck, pass me that bottle!"

See page 52.

2 Poop a loop.

Mom: Oh, my fucking god! Dad come and look,

Fog did it again. −Insanely screams.

Dad: What's the problem? −Walks into the

bathroom where she is standing holding her breath.

Mom: First my rugs, now in the tub? Do you know

how many mismatched bathroom rugs I have, tons!

Dad: Well at least it was not the kitchen or on the

bed, you know he may be a sleepwalker… I have

watched him walking out in the middle of the night.

Mom: Why haven't you said something and what are you doing awake so late?

Dad: 3:33 am, I called it the message time but that's not what matters now, hey, probably he doesn't like the toilet.

Mom: I don't care, he needs to start acting like a grown up and do things properly, I'm tired of cleaning all the mess you two leave behind.

Dad: You were the one who wanted a child.

−Mumbling.

Mom: The fuck you say?

Dad: I mean we love Fog and we must be patient and supportive.

Mom: Patient my ass, you clean this up! −Walks away, giving him a scrub and bleach.

Dad: It's just poop, you almost made me drop my

beer…

Fog: I'm home! −Door noise.

Mom: Fog, I need to talk to you about the tub.

Fog: Oh, about that, you know I think dad is a

sleepwalker. −Said quietly.

See page 53.

3

Google abattoirs on images.

Fog: Mom! –Shouts so stunned.

Mom: What! I'm just behind you. –Dad sights.

Fog: What the fuck is this? There's someone's foot in my soup, my appetite is ruined.

Dad: Fog you been asking your mom for that soup all month long. –Calmly says.

Fog: Yeah for a chicken soup but this, it's like you are feeding me corpses.

Mom: Son you are kidding, right?

Fog: Sorry I don't want to be an asshole, but is there any burgers left from last night?

Mom: Oh, so now you want to eat the rest of the cow. −Sarcastically smiles at him.

Fog: Alright stop it! Does that mean every menu we have ate has being made with dead animals, I though the meat came from a happy place like the box says, I even though the cows were part of the crew like in charge of supervising the miraculously handmade patties and the chickens donated their breast since it grows back, tell me I'm right.

Mom: Well no, they come directly from a slaughter house! Those poor animals, that's why we became vegetarians eight years ago but don't worry we are not that bad, in China they eat dogs, frogs and rats.

Fog: That is disgusting! And you wanted me to learn Chinese, ah! −His eyes in shock. −I see we were going to move to China, so you can eat me there and no one would ever stop it.

Mom: I think you are over reacting. −Chewing on avocado fries.

Fog: You don't know me mother! From now on we won't consume any products made in China.

Dad: Wow everything is made there even this house was made in China. −Opening his arms.

Fog: It is okay father, I'm going to be living in the backyard until we rebuild.

Mom: Don't forget the trash on your way out!

Dad: it will take a while, son!

Fog: Go local!

See page 54.

4

Guffaw.

Fog and two of his best friends were having lunch at a local downtown market and without inhibitions they laugh uncontrollably.

Fog: I can't believe we forgot to bring Mike to his birthday lunch. −Between laughs, he mumbles.

Mom: Is that you son? −She stands up from one of the near tables then approach the group.

Fog: Well, what are you both doing here?

−Referring to his parents.

Dad: You always talk about this place, so we are giving it a chance, are these your friends?

Fog: Yes dad, their names are Michael and Miguel, part of the mikes!

−They both say hi at the same time.

Mom: Hi boys, I always wanted to meet you, he told us a lot of good things about you.

Dad: Yeah, the mike's one gay, one straight and the other, Is that beer? −Mouthwatering.

Miguel: Yes, and I don't share so let's grab one for you. −Both walk to a beer stand.

Michael: So, what about you honey?

Mom: Oh, thanks, I don't drink beer, well unless there's no other option.

Michael: Omg! Sweetie let me grab a mimosa for you, they are delicious!

Mom: Wow son you impressed me today, it seems your father and I, have been doing a good job.

Michael: Here you go, Carlos makes the best mimosas, did you notice how fast he delivers?

Mom: Not as fast as Fog's father! −Laughs out loud.

Dad: Well I have one pool table at home, son your friends are amazing, you guys should visit us.

Mom: I think the same way about them too.

Dad: You are so welcome at our home, hey! What about this Saturday if you guys have nothing to do. So, I can show you my UFO collection.

Michael: Sounds good to me, omg I can bring some exquisite rose wine I ordered straight from Italy, you are going to love it, and if it's ok, may I bring Charline?

Mom: Sure, we have a big yard for your poodle!

Michael: Oh, Charline is not my poodle, she is my wife!

Mom: Wait, what? Aren't you the gay? —Surprised she spits her drink out.

Miguel: No, he is the straight and I am the gay!

Dad: What are you talking about?

Fog: Please don't embarrass me. Mom, dad, this is Michael "the straight" and Miguel "the gay".

Mom: Of course! I knew it, its just that you are so Sweet. —Replies with a connotating tone.

Dad: Man, you rock, I love you! —Everyone turns to dad. —He is attractive, what you want me to say?

Fog: Dad!

See page 55.

5

Bar Hopping.

Fog wakes up, opens his eyes and stares at the ceiling, after his birthday celebration, him and the mikes wake up in a spacious hotel room all three covered in chocolate.

Fog: Fuck, my head! It's going to explode!

Miguel: Dude I can barely move. –When he tries to stand up the sound of cracks fill the room.

Fog: Ha, man you are covered in white, you stupid.

Miguel: Hey, Michael wake up fool. –Throwing a pillow to him.

Michael: Oh, Charline I need some chamomile tea… wait, omg this is chocolate! Oh well I heard is good for the skin.

Fog: What the fuck did we do last night? –Stands up and walks to the mirror.

–A moment of panic raised his heart beats, when he realizes all of them were nude covered in white chocolate but their mouths and private parts with messy dark chocolate.

Fog: My fucking god! Do not tell me we sucked each other's dicks! –Paranoia reaction.

Michael: It's not that bad, this chocolate is tasty!

Miguel: Dude, did I make out with you two! I'm going to puke; you guys are totally not my type. I am gay, and I got standards!

−Suddenly a door opens, and four people walk out all covered in dark chocolate with messy white chocolate on their mouths and private parts.

Oh baby, you were amazing! so sad your friends fall asleep early. −First lady.

Honey, I will never, ever forget you! −Second lady.

Mm, papi I'll be waiting for your call! −Third lady.

That was awesome! −A guy.

Fog: What's going on?

Guy: You guys clearly started the game but fall asleep before the big act.

Obviously, we were hungry. −Second lady.

By the way happy birthday! Birthday boy. −First lady.

Ay, gracias for your friend. −Third lady.

Mike: Fuckers I'm the man! –Third mike yells from the room.

Fog: Wow, so that means we didn't make out!

Miguel: Thanks, dear saint Juan Gabriel!

Michael: Oh no, that's so unfortunate!

–Everybody turns to see Michael.

See page 56.

6 Sibling.

Fog: So, let me ask you again, why haven't you guys have any more children?

Mom: Well let's say we have enough with other people's kids.

Fog: So, what about me? Do you hate me too?

Mom: For fog's sake, no! You are different.

Dad: True, you work, you clean after yourself and soon you are moving out of the house to go to Florida, right?

Fog: Yeah! I guess it was a stupid question, think I just overheard my aunt Lucero.

Mom: What did that bitch say?

Fog: Calm down mom, she is your sister.

Mom: And she still a bitch! I get it now… she is mad because her kid was playing with the salt and pepper making a mess and I kindly offer a toy instead, so she got pissed! She asked me if I hated her son? I don't hate my nephew… I fucking hate HER! Because she is the grown up, she should know better. This is not her house, she must respect and be conscious about keeping everything the way it is. I mean we invited her over to have a good time but I'm not going to clean after her kid's mess, and she still got upset! That fucking bitch! I mean yes, I was going to clean the table, wash the dishes and just continue having a fucking good time! But why

should I be worried about refilling the salt and

pepper again?

Fog: Ok mom, I get it!

Mom: Do you Fog? Do you?

See page 57.

7 Otaku.

Dad: Oh no, why?

Fog: What's going on? –Runs to the living room.

Dad: Why are you doing this to me?

Fog: Mom, what's happening? Are you two getting a divorce?

Dad: No! I can't take it no more.

Fog: Are you hurt? Oh, are you dying dad? Is that what it is?

Mom: Stop! You will get over this soon! Son we are not getting a divorce and yes, he is going to die, I mean we all going to die someday, right? Your dad

is upset because they cancel his TV show again and

it may take another year or two, for the new season.

Dad: What if I die before the next season start? I

have waited for over 20 years!

Fog: Is this for real dad? I mean there are worst

things happening in the world right now and you are

having a tantrum over a cartoon?

Dad: It's not a cartoon Fog, it's call Anime!

Fog: I still think it's absurd.

Dad: Oh yeah, well Fog let me tell you something,

you are still not allowed to be off leash in any of the

California coast beaches except for your favorite

place Rosie's beach, you bitch!

Fog: Oh! Well fuck you too! –Fog runs back to his

room crying.

Mom: You son of a bitch!

Dad: I'm sorry darling, sorry Fog!

Mom: You're dumb, I was saving that line for my own satisfaction. Son, mommy is coming!

See page 58.

8

Griffith the teetotaler.

Fog: Wow, she is so beautiful! –Watching a girl, on a trail while hiking.

Michael: I can't look, I'm faithful to Charline!

Miguel: Yeah, she seems nice.

Fog: Nice? Dude she is hot! let's see if my "get a girl" line still works.

Girl: Hi, omg I love your glasses! –She says before him, then smiles.

Fog: Thanks, I just came to say, uh. –Is interrupted by her friends.

Girl: Oh, here are my friends! Maria and Mariah!

Fog: What a coincidence, my friends are Miguel
and Michael and my name is Fog, what's your
name?

Girl: Wai.

Fog: Because, I already introduce myself and I
would like to date you?

Girl: Wai. –She repeats kind of upset.

Fog: Because we love hiking in L.A., I mean don't
you think we have a lot in common your friend's
names are so similar and so are my friend's names,
by any chance is one of them lesbian?

Mariah: Yes, asshole is me, for your info she
answered your question and said Wai.

Fog: Because I want to know her name!

Miguel: Fog, shut up man! –Throws a rock to him.

Fog: Yes, but Why?

Girl: Yes, Wai!

Fog: Now she is mocking me!

Girl: No silly! My name is Wai not Why.

Fog: Oh so, it happens to me too you know, Fog and Fuck.

See page 59.

9 Procrastination.

Fog: Mom, have you seen my violin?

Mom: Your dad sold it!

Fog: Why? It was mine.

Mom: Probably he did, since you haven't play with it, like 2 years ago when he bought it for you.

—One hour later.

Fog: Mom, have you seen my electrical piano?

Mom: He sold it too, 4 years ago, when you started the bartending school.

Fog: What about my Italian and Japanese easy learn programs, or my tennis racquet, the paddle board, my set of yoga, my easel and canvas, did he sell them too?

Mom: Oh yeah, Fog you would of been a great polymath, but your eagerness to learn new things distract you from completing one goal and then moving to the next task, you may think you are multitasking but I would say it's more of a dream and goals hoarder, I think you should see an specialist and work this issue.

Fog: Ok mom, so let's go together, so we can get rid of all the news paper and magazines you accumulated over time, we cannot use the living room no more, you are a compulsive hoarder!

Mom: You piece of shit, your stuff is in the garage! And I am not a hoarder I just like to keep those for future references, that's all.

Fog: Sure, what about the cat? Do you remember what happen to him? He died mom, crushed under a pile of heavy books! And now that we talk about it, I haven't seen my dad in a couple of days.

Dad: Help! I fell and can't get up... −With a tired voice.

Mom: Got it! Everything must go, don't look at me like that Fog. Here we come husbando!

See page 60.

10 He has a Milo face!

Dad: We ate like pigs. –Finishing dinner at home.

Fog: I am so stuffed! Got to take a walk.

Mom: Sure honey, not you dad, you will help with the dishes!

–Fog goes for a walk and later returns with a two-year-old kid.

Fog: I'm back and look what I found on the street.

Mom: what the hell is that?

Dad: Holy shoe, can we keep him! Please!

Mom: No, he has a family, he looks clean and has a bracelet, it says he is lactose intolerant and O negative type blood.

Fog: Wonder what his name is? I already tried Romy, Mondray, Tony, Cody and Felipe but the only one he responds to is Milo, so let's call him that! Milo!

Mom: Don't you think we should call the police now?

Dad: For what? These parents are so irresponsible! It's raining and it's cold outside; we should teach them a lesson, this baby stays with us tonight, plus he seems to like us. –Making funny faces.

Fog: Dad is right! What if we keep him forever?

Mom: What? And stop living my life and dreams, I mean his family probably misses him.

Fog: What if he ran away and we are his only salvation.

Dad: I just hope it's not your kid.

Fog: What? Where that come from?

Dad: all I'm saying is accidents happen and they become a pain in the ass.

Fog: So, what you are saying is, I was a mistake!

Mom: Alright, we thought you were bad luck at first but then we found out we hit jackpot.

Fog: How's that?

Mom: Taxes.

Fog: Are you kidding me?

Mom: Hey, having kids is a gold mine for a lot of folks, not for us, we are ok with the crumbs.

Kid: You are all crazy!

–Everyone turns to the little one.

Fog: You can talk.

Kid: Ah, yeah! My name is Riley not Milo, I thought my family was a mess, but I see there are worst, I can't stand you all.

Mom: well look at that!

Kid: I'm bored, later. –Walking out the door.

Fog: Wait up kiddo! Do you like cake? We got a "pastel de tres leches" which is Spanish for triple wonder maker.

Kid: I guess it is the least I could have after listening to you all. – walks out eating the cake.

Dad: That little bastard!

Mom: And you wanted to keep him forever, huh?

Fog: Are we really that bad of a family?

Dad: Because of the cake? No, I don't think so.

See page 61.

11 Do you hear me?

The phone rings at Fog's job

Fog: Hello.

Caller: Hi Sr. I am calling from southern California energy company and our records show that your bill hasn't been paid and one of our technicians is going now to your business to disconnect the service.

Fog: Who the fuck didn't pay the electric bill?

–Yelling out loud in the office. –Listen man I'm not in charge of that, let me give you the accountant's phone number, okay?

Jenna: Hey Fog, I think it's a scam call again.

–Coworker advises, and Fog winks at her.

Caller: Uh sr. I'm not a male, I am a female!

Fog: Well I didn't ask for your gender, right? Listen this is a busy place and we work hard to get money the right way, not scamming people around, you fucking mother fucker!

Caller: Sr. you are mistaken.

Fog: Mistaken my ass! Karma is a fucking bitch, and the universe is watching. You think you are smart, but life is going to prove you wrong, fucking piece of shit! –Hangs the phone.

Jenna: Fog, you are my hero!

Fog: Anytime!

–Once they turn themselves back to work the power goes off.

Jenna: I guess they didn't really pay the bill.

Fog: I guess Jenna.

See page 62.

12 The coolest neighborhood.

First drink of the night.

Fog: Ok, so is this the place?

Miguel: Yeah, they say here you can get a match
even without any dating apps.

Second drink of the night.

Fog: Do you trust?

Miguel: No, I'm on Grindere already.

Fog: I'm on Tindere too.

Third drink of the night.

Miguel: I mean I don't get it, I'm almost perfect but still single, its like people are allergic to perfection.

Fog: I know, I got the perfect life, job and goals but these girls keep on choosing the jerks!

Fourth cocktail of the night.

Miguel: I don't want to be a wing man forever, I want a man for my own!

Fog: Do I have a best friend sign over my head? Cause all the girls find me adorable but not lovable.

Fifth cocktail of the night.

Miguel: Man, what are we doing here?

Fog: We want soulmates! And we want them now!

Sixth cocktail of the night.

Miguel: Dude, what are we drinking? I want to puke!

Fog: No, no, no, no don't puke… someone may

Kiss you tonight.

Seventh drink of the night.

Miguel: Everybody is dancing and I'm not, I'm here

stuck with you.

Fog: I'm getting fucked up.

Eighth drink of the night.

Miguel: This shit is boring, let's go to a strip club!

Fog: Like, like a girl strip club?

Miguel: Yeah bro, it's your night!

Fog: No man, let's go to WEHO, let's have fun!

Bartender: Another round of Adios motherfucker,

amigos?

Wait, what? –Both puke at the same time.

See page 63.

13 Dr. Felicia.

Mom: Fog hurry up, didn't I say, do not get in the lake, gosh, when are you going to listen to me?

Fog: Mom, I feel horrible.

Dad: Like father, like son, huh?

Dr. Felicia: Omg, you look awful, what's going on?

Mom: Well, here Mr. show off got drunk and jumped in the water in fucking Big Bear Lake and it was snowing, could you believe that?

Fog: Mom, you are not helping.

Dr. Felicia: Are you taking something right now?

Mom: Home remedies, vegetable soup and a shot of tequila with extra lime juice, you know, vitamin c.

Dr. Felicia: Are you serious? That is not medicine, how long have you been sick?

Fog: It started three days ago.

Mom: Please don't think I am a bad parent, I tried to bring him to the ER last night, but guess what, Fog doesn't like to stay in the hospital.

Fog: It gives me the creeps!

Mom: Being wasted in snow land, for fog's sake.

Dr. Felicia: And to all of this where were you madam at the time?

Fog: Yeah, mom tell her.

Mom: I was recording him. −Avoiding eye contact.

Fog: Bingo! And she was wasted too.

Dr. Felicia: You guys should be careful, alcohol and swimming don't go together, it's dangerous.

Dad: I believe ordering a whiskey with diet cola, just don't go together, have you heard something more outrageous than that? I don't think so, we all know mixing alcohol with diet soda get you drunk way faster, but to what price? Diet soda tastes nasty! Not for me thanks.

Dr. Felicia: Let me guess you are the father.

Dad: That's what Mr. Springy said. −Laughs.

Fog: Dad!

Dr. Felicia: Here, this will help you with the cold.

Fog: That was fast! Thanks Doctor, shut up mom.

Dr. Felicia: No problem, you three be safe!

Mom: Likewise, bye Felicia! −Walking away.

Fog: Mom!

Mom: What? That is her name, and another check off my bucket list!

Dad: I see, I'm impressed.

Fog: How come?

Mom: Well, I always wanted to say bye to an actual person named Felicia and I did!

Fog: Gosh, we are going to hell.

Dad: Not me, my vital energy goes back to the universe.

Fog: It's an expression, dad.

See page 64.

Things unpublished

1

Fog the Dog was inspired by Kosmo, my four-ledge

son who was born in Florida June 15th, 2012. The

idea of this project was conceived while walking

Kosmo on a foggy morning in Los Angeles CA,

December 31st, 2017.

As "The mission" mentions mezcal has become one

of my favorites for cocktails because of the smoky

taste, making your drinks beautifully tasty.

2

We do live in an apartment building and believe it or not, Kosmo has never done his needs in the carpet. Although when he has been sick or cannot hold it any longer, he will go to the restroom and do it on a bath rug then he folds it neatly as a burrito, yes, I have a few mismatched bath rugs, let's call it "poop a loop".

3

To be honest, Kosmo is super spoiled, one day
(since he loves chicken) I cooked some chicken feet
thinking he will eat it, I was so wrong! He gave me
one of his "you annoy me so much" looks, so I
never did it again.

"Google abattoirs on images" it's also my own call
to stop consuming animal products, since it is
hypocrite to try to stop the ruthless assassination of
dogs in China and so the cruel way fur companies
peel animals alive for merchandise.

4

"Guffaw" is what you do with your family and friends while having a good time, Kosmo loves great places with awesome atmosphere and pet friendly like Grant Central Market in Downtown, mimosas, beer and oysters? Dude.

This project is a, let's make sure a motherfucker understands, there is only one race "Human".

5

Yes, Kosmo loves Vegas too. He is the best wing man, just saying. He has followed me to some "Bar hopping" adventures, good drinks, good food and great company.

Facts:

−Alcohol is bad for dogs.

−Chocolate is bad for dogs.

−Love is the best option for dogs.

6

There is a quote that says: Don't ask, don't tell!

Well let me tell you, "Sibling" it's intended for

people who still got confused with the words

"service" and "slavery", if your kid plays with the

sugar packets or the salt and pepper shakers, it's not

their fault but yours, so bring some toys like Kosmo

does, and biodegradable poop bags!

7

"Otaku" not only refers to the amazing world of anime but also to the crazy idea of not creating new dog friendly off leash beaches in California. Meanwhile Kosmo will keep his attendance to "Rosie's beach" in Long Beach and me finding awesome new anime series, please tag me in.

8

Yes, we can agree alcoholism is a serious problem,

remember anything in excess is bad.

Whenever we have a chance, we go on a hike at

Jenkins place, Griffith Park. Always sober!

And so, number eight belongs to "Griffith the

Teetotaler".

9

Procrastination (from Latin's "procrastinare", that translates in to: the prefix pro-, 'forward', and the suffix -crastinus, 'till next day' from cras, 'tomorrow') is the avoidance of doing a task that needs to be accomplished. Sometimes, procrastination takes place until the "last minute" before a deadline. Procrastination can take hold on any aspect of life— putting off cleaning the stove, repairing a leaky roof, seeing a doctor or dentist, submitting a job report or academic assignment or breaching a stressful issue with a partner. Procrastination can lead to feelings of guilt, inadequacy, depression, and self-doubt.

By Wikipedia.

10

How important is to microchip your pet?

Dude, important!

Earlier this year we found, (later we knew his name

was Riley) a super cute friendly dog in the street,

"He has a Milo face". Next day reunited with his

family.

Cannot imagine how desperate, anxious and stress

the lost pets may feel, they can't communicate in

human words so love your pet and microchip

her/him, be responsible!

Yes, tres leches cake contains dairy.

11

How many scam calls have you receive in the past?

Be careful and never answer the phone with a yes,

be smart.

Damn it, I should have asked you differently, let's

try again.

−Are you cute?

   a)   Yes.−Scammed, you are Fog!

   b)   No. −Good job!

"Do you hear me?"

   a)   Español, por favor.

   b)   Français s'il vous plaît.

−Never with a yes.

12

"The coolest neighborhood in LA" it's always fun
and we know why, because we are cool!

13

"Dr. Felicia" it's a fictitious named I create putting together the first letter of my best favorite food also contains the best ingredients for happiness and love and adding... just fucking kidding, she was the first person who helped me at Kosmo's vets. Hi Felicia!

Shout-out to Francisco de Santiago!

Fog says: You are the man!

Follow me on Instagram @doghuman.la

Use the hashtags #forfogssake #fogthedog

Contact me fogthedogbook@gmail.com

Don't forget to tag me for pet friendly places in

L.A. Kosmo always in the mood to go out.

66

www.ingramcontent.com/pod-product-compliance
Lightning Source LLC
Chambersburg PA
CBHW071429040426
42445CB00012BA/1315